DEAR ME

Letters to Myself, For All of My Emotions

Written by Donna Tetreault and Illustrated by Elisena Bonadio

ISBN Hardcover: 978-0-578-81236-6 / ISBN Paperback: 978-1-7364798-0-3 / ISBN eBook: 978-1-7364798-1-0

First edition 2021

Published in the United States of America

Printed in the United States of America

For Jackson and Asher,
Always be true to the inside of you!
Love, Mom

GLOOMY

CURIOUS

LOVED

PLEASED

CHEERFUL

ASHAMED

BUBBLY

THANKFUL

GRUMPY

FOCUSED

SHY

MIGHTY

I am a happy little boy.
Most of the time.

I can also be...

EXCITED	PEACEFUL	SURPRISED

SAD	MAD	BORED

SCARED	JOYFUL	**FRUSTRATED**

Mom says the many ways that I feel are called emotions,
and that it's okay to feel every single one of them.
She tells me it's okay for everyone in our family to feel their emotions.

I feel good when I'm happy or excited.
But I don't like being sad or scared.
Mom says she understands.

She wants to teach me how to think about my emotions in a new way.
A pencil and paper is how we start.

Mom says writing my feelings down is one way to feel my emotions.
I just have to write what's in my heart.
And I can manage how I feel.
It's up to me.

It's a brand new day.
The sun is shining.
I'm going to play at the park.

Today I am **EXCITED**!

It's the first day at a new school.
I'm afraid to meet my teacher.
What if I don't make any friends?

Today I am scared.

DEAR ME,

It's okay to be scared. Mom says my teacher will be kind and that I'll make new friends.
It just takes some time and practice to feel comfortable.

LOVE,
ME

This morning Dad left for a work trip.
He will be gone for three days.
I will miss him so much.

Today I am **SAD**.

DEAR ME,

It's natural to be sad. And I know Dad has to work. I really, truly do.
Mom says I'll see him Friday afternoon, and he'll take me to the bookstore.

LOVE,
ME

I reach for Mom's hand when we visit Grandma at the hospital.
It's cold here and I have to be quiet.

Today I am worried.

DEAR ME,

Feeling worried is just another one of my emotions. Mom says she's worried too. It's okay for us to feel this way.

We can take deep breaths to feel better. Breathe in and out. Breathe in and out.

Breathe in and out.

LOVE,
ME

During soccer practice, we have to stop playing to take team pictures.
I want to play soccer right now.
I don't like having my picture taken.

Today I am **MAD!**

My best friend in the whole wide world is sad because his goldfish died.
He cries.
I hug him.
He has emotions too.

Today I am kind to others.

I want to swing high on the swings at the playground.
I want to feel like a bird flying.
I fall off.
Will kids laugh at me?
Will anyone help?

Today I feel embarrassed and **SURPRISED**.

DEAR ME,

One kid laughs, but it's okay.
Another helps pick me up. She smiles big and says,
"You like being high in the sky!"
I like when kids choose to be kind.

LOVE,
ME

It's Taco Salad Tuesday.
Again!
I don't like taco salad!
I like regular old tacos!
Can't we just have Taco Tuesday?
Minus the salad!

Today I am **frustrated**.

DEAR ME,
Mom says she understands I am frustrated.
But she explains she wants me to enjoy healthy meals too.
    She makes a deal. Tacos ONLY next Tuesday.
        LOVE,
        ME

I love bath time!
My brother and I laugh.
We splish.
We splash.
We make lots of bubbles.

Today I am **joyful!**

DEAR ME,

I wish we could stay in the bath
way past bedtime.
This is our special time.
Today we made our first
bubble inside a bubble. So cool!

LOVE,
ME

It's raining outside.
I like watching the rain.
Mom says it's a good time to relax and get cozy.
I will count the raindrops that fall on my window.

Today I am **peaceful**.

DEAR ME,

I lose count of all the raindrops. So now I just listen...
drip, drop, drip, drop, drip, drop.
I start to collect my 'Dear Me' letters.

LOVE,
ME

Now is the perfect time to show Mom all of my letters.
I tell her that I understand that all of my emotions are what make me, me.

Mom agrees!
She says she is very proud and gives me a big hug.
I AM PROUD OF MYSELF, TOO.
I know I can manage my emotions any time I want.
All I have to do is start with DEAR ME.

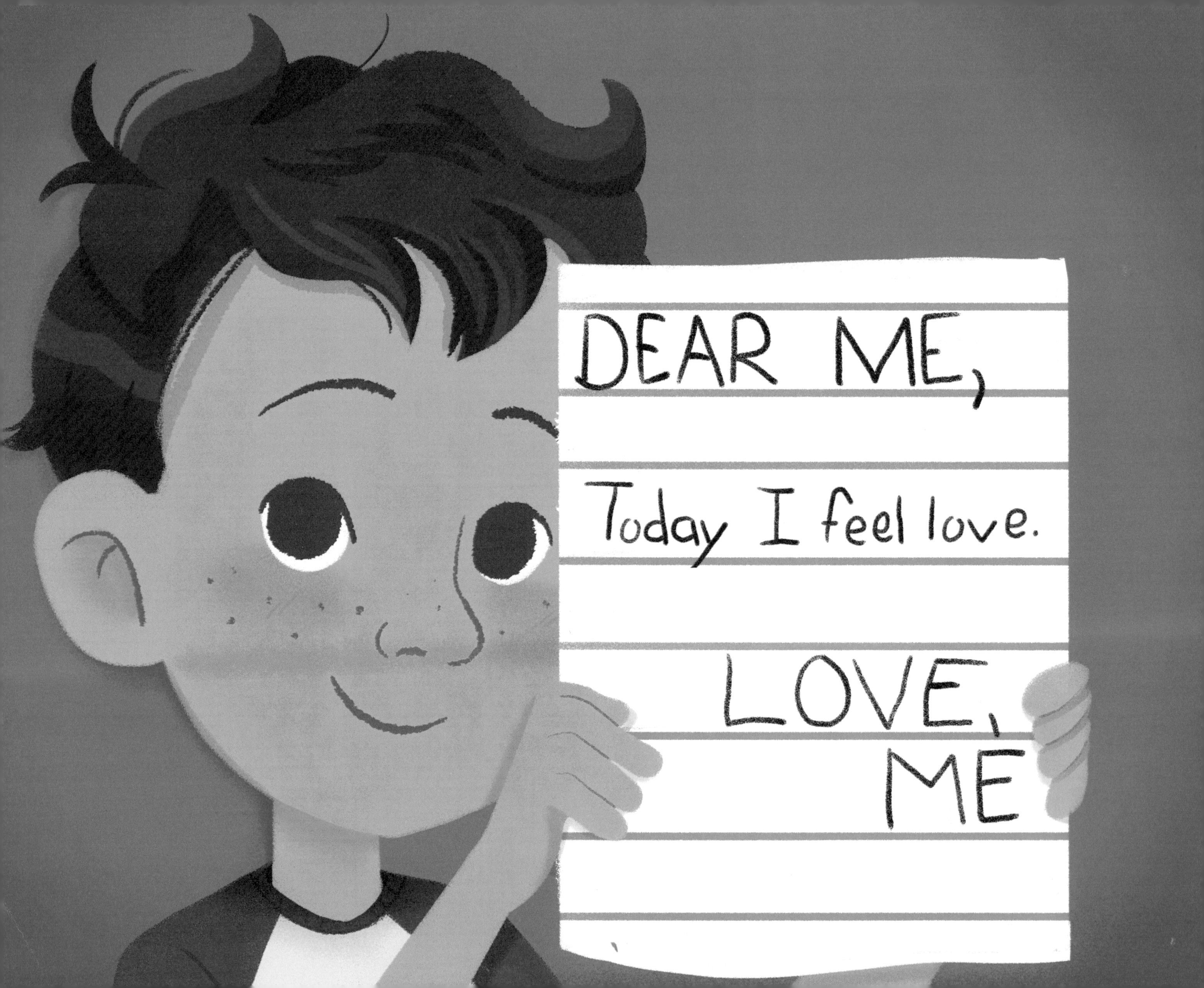
DEAR ME,
Today I feel love.
LOVE,
ME

DONNA TETREAULT is a national TV parenting journalist, seen on *Dr. Phil, The Doctors, The Today Show* and *200 Nexstar Stations* across the country on her weekly parenting segment, 'Kids Under Construction.' She is also a *Thrive Global Contributor*, educator, and nonprofit founder.

Her debut children's book, *Dear Me, Letters to Myself For All of My Emotions* is a Readers' Favorite Award Winner in the Educational Category. *Dear Me* proactively teaches children positive mental health strategies. Her parenting book, *The C.A.S.T.L.E. Method: Building a Family Foundation on Compassion, Acceptance, Security, Trust, Love, and Expectations plus Education* will be released by Familius/Hachette May 2022.

ELISENA BONADIO is a California-based illustrator. In 2018, she graduated from the Arts University Bournemouth with a degree in animation, but the following year was drawn into the fun and vibrant world of children's illustration. Since then, she has illustrated picture books, coloring pages, and chapter books.

FOCUSED

GRUMPY

SILLY

MIGHTY

BRAVE

GLOOMY

CPSIA information can be obtained
at www.ICGtesting.com
Printed in the USA
BVRC100820251021
619814BV00002B/3